Contents

A Review of CBO's Activities in 2014 Under the Unfunded Mandates Reform Act

The federal government, through laws and regulations, sometimes imposes requirements—known as federal mandates—on state, local, and tribal governments and entities in the private sector to achieve national goals. In 1995, lawmakers enacted the Unfunded Mandates Reform Act (UMRA) in part to ensure that, during the legislative process, the Congress receives information about the potential effects of mandates as it considers proposed legislation. To that end, UMRA requires the Congressional Budget Office, at certain stages in the legislative process, to assess the cost of mandates that would apply to state, local, and tribal governments or to the private sector. This report, which is part of an annual series that began in 1997, summarizes CBO's activities in 2014 under UMRA.

How Is a Mandate Defined in UMRA?

UMRA defines a mandate as any provision in legislation that, when enacted, would do one of the following:

- Impose an enforceable duty on state, local, or tribal governments or on private-sector entities;[1]

- Reduce or eliminate an authorization of appropriations to cover the costs of complying with existing mandates;

- Increase the stringency of conditions that apply to the provision of funds to state, local, or tribal governments through certain large mandatory programs or make cuts in federal funding for those mandatory programs if the affected governments lack the flexibility to alter the programs.

Duties that arise from conditions of federal assistance or that are tied to participating in voluntary federal programs generally are not considered mandates as defined in UMRA.

What Does UMRA Require of CBO?

The law requires CBO to prepare mandate statements for bills and joint resolutions that are approved by authorizing committees.[2] When requested, the agency also reviews legislation at other stages in the legislative process for intergovernmental and private-sector mandates.[3] As a part of its review of legislation, CBO must determine whether the aggregate direct costs of the mandates would be greater than the statutory thresholds established in UMRA and identify any funding that the bill would provide to cover those costs.[4] (See Appendix A for details about CBO's responsibilities under UMRA and for an overview of the law's other provisions.) In 2014, the thresholds, which are adjusted annually for inflation, were $76 million for intergovernmental mandates and $152 million for private-sector mandates.[5]

How Many Bills Reviewed by CBO in 2014 Contained Mandates?

CBO found that most of the legislation the Congress considered in 2014 contained no mandates as defined in UMRA. Of the 539 bills CBO reviewed in 2014,

---

1. UMRA does not define the term "enforceable duty," but CBO has interpreted it to mean actions by public and private entities that would be either required or prohibited.

2. Authorizing committees have legislative jurisdiction over the establishment, continuation, and operation of federal programs or agencies and the authorization of appropriations for them.

3. Legislation includes amendments, bills introduced in or acts passed by the House or Senate, and conference reports. For simplicity, this report refers to legislation reviewed by CBO during the legislative process collectively as bills.

4. The staff of the Joint Committee on Taxation examines tax provisions of legislation to identify federal mandates and estimates their costs. CBO's mandate statements incorporate such information.

5. The intergovernmental and private-sector thresholds established in UMRA were $50 million and $100 million, respectively, in 1996.

47, or 9 percent, contained intergovernmental mandates and 75, or 14 percent, contained private-sector mandates. Both percentages are lower than the averages for the 2010–2013 period, which were 13 percent for intergovernmental mandates and 16 percent for private-sector mandates. Most of the mandates that CBO identified in 2014 would not have imposed costs that exceeded the thresholds. Only 4 bills included an intergovernmental mandate with estimated costs above the threshold, and 12 bills contained private-sector mandates that would have imposed costs that were estimated to exceed the threshold.

Occasionally, CBO cannot determine whether the cost of the mandates in a bill would exceed the annual cost thresholds. In most such cases, the reason for that conclusion is uncertainty about the scope of a mandate—the number of people or entities affected, the extent of the requirements they would face, or both. Such uncertainty generally arises because of insufficient information about how a federal agency would implement the provisions of the bill. For example, legislation often gives a federal agency broad discretion in issuing regulations, and without information on the scope of the regulations to be issued, CBO cannot estimate with any confidence the cost of the bill's requirements at such an early stage. In 2014, CBO could not determine the annual costs of private-sector mandates in 9 bills (less than 2 percent of the bills reviewed).

How Many Public Laws Enacted in 2014 Contain Mandates?

In addition to examining bills during the legislative process, CBO reviews public laws enacted each year for intergovernmental and private-sector mandates. Of the 224 public laws enacted in 2014, 16 (7 percent) contain intergovernmental mandates, none of which are mandates estimated to have costs that exceed the intergovernmental threshold. Twenty-six of the laws enacted in 2014 (12 percent) contain private-sector mandates; five of those laws include mandates estimated to have costs that exceed the private-sector threshold. Those five laws contain five private-sector mandates: Three extended government fees; one extended a requirement on insurers to cover health care provided by the Department of Veterans Affairs for conditions related to military service; and one regulated a set of pharmaceutical compounds as anabolic steroids.

In the 19 years since UMRA became effective, CBO has identified only 13 laws with intergovernmental mandates that have costs estimated to exceed the statutory threshold and 97 laws with private-sector mandates that have costs

estimated to exceed the threshold (including the 5 laws enacted in 2014).

How Is This Report Organized?

The tables in this report provide information about mandates that were enacted between 2010 and 2014 or that CBO reviewed in legislation considered during that period, with a particular focus on legislation enacted or considered in 2014:

- Table 1 on page 3 is a tally of mandates in public laws enacted between 2010 and 2014;

- Table 2 on page 4 shows the number of mandate statements CBO transmitted between 2010 and 2014, and the number of those for which the estimated costs exceeded the thresholds specified in UMRA;

- Tables 3 and 4 (on pages 5 and 8) list laws enacted in 2014 that contain intergovernmental and private-sector mandates, respectively;

- Tables 5 and 6 (on pages 14 and 15) list intergovernmental and private-sector mandates, respectively, that CBO identified in 2014 as having costs that would exceed UMRA's thresholds or that could not be determined; and

- Tables 7 and 8 (on pages 17 and 24) list legislation CBO reviewed in 2014 that contained intergovernmental and private-sector mandates, respectively.

Although data for spending and receipts in the budget are presented for fiscal years, which run from October 1 through September 30, Congressional sessions generally follow the calendar year; therefore, data on CBO's cost estimates and mandate statements are presented as calendar year totals.

The number of bills that contain mandates and the number of individual mandates that appear in proposed legislation generally differ. Because the House and the Senate may consider the same or similar mandates in more than one piece of legislation, the number of bills that contain mandates can be greater than the number of individual mandates considered by the Congress in any given year. Conversely, because one bill may contain several mandates, the number of mandates identified can be greater than the number of bills reviewed.

Table 1.

Laws Enacted Between 2010 and 2014 That Contain Mandates

In 2014, 224 public laws were enacted. Sixteen of those laws contain at least one intergovernmental mandate as defined in the Unfunded Mandates Reform Act (UMRA), and 26 contain one or more private-sector mandates. A total of 24 intergovernmental mandates and 55 private-sector mandates were enacted.

The Congressional Budget Office determined that none of the intergovernmental mandates enacted in 2014 have costs that will exceed the statutory threshold established in UMRA ($76 million in 2014) or have costs that could not be determined.

The public laws enacted in 2014 contain five private-sector mandates with annual costs that, in CBO's estimation, will exceed the statutory threshold established in UMRA ($152 million in 2014). CBO could not determine whether the costs for three of the private-sector mandates enacted in 2014 will be above or below the statutory threshold.

	2010 [a]	2011	2012	2013	2014
	Intergovernmental Mandates				
Laws That Contain Mandates	29	12	16	3	16
Total Mandates Enacted	**86**	**23**	**44**	**4**	**24**
Mandates with costs that exceed the statutory threshold	7	0	0	0	0
Mandates with costs that could not be determined	7	0	1	0	0
Mandates with costs that fall below the statutory threshold	72	23	43	4	24
	Private-Sector Mandates				
Laws That Contain Mandates	50	16	23	8	26
Total Mandates Enacted	**129**	**51**	**75**	**18**	**55**
Mandates with costs that exceed the statutory threshold	25	7	12	5	5
Mandates with costs that could not be determined	21	1	16	1	3
Mandates with costs that fall below the statutory threshold	83	43	47	12	47

Source: Congressional Budget Office.

Note: The thresholds established in UMRA for intergovernmental and private-sector mandates were $50 million and $100 million, respectively, in 1996. UMRA specifies that the statutory thresholds be adjusted each year for inflation. In 2014, the statutory thresholds for intergovernmental and private-sector mandates were $76 million and $152 million, respectively.

a. A significant number of the mandates enacted into law in 2010 were related to the Patient Protection and Affordable Care Act (Public Law 111-148) and the Dodd-Frank Wall Street Reform and Consumer Protection Act (P.L. 111-203). A full listing of all mandates enacted into law since 1996 that had estimated costs exceeding the thresholds established in UMRA can be found in Appendix B.

Table 2.

Mandate Statements Transmitted by CBO, 2010 to 2014

The Congressional Budget Office provides mandate statements to the Congress for most of the bills that are reported by authorizing committees. CBO also prepares mandate statements for proposed amendments and other bills as requested and to the extent practicable. Most of that legislation is never enacted.

In 2014, CBO reviewed 539 bills, of which 47, or 9 percent, contained intergovernmental mandates and 75, or 14 percent, contained private-sector mandates. By comparison, the averages for the 2010–2013 period were 13 percent (for intergovernmental mandates) and 16 percent (for private-sector mandates).

In 2014, the statutory thresholds established in the Unfunded Mandates Reform Act (UMRA) for intergovernmental and private-sector mandates were $76 million and $152 million, respectively. Of the legislation CBO analyzed last year, only 4 bills (less than 1 percent) included intergovernmental mandates with costs estimated to exceed the threshold, and 12 bills (about 2 percent) contained private-sector mandates with such costs. Unlike in previous years, none of the legislation analyzed in 2014 contained intergovernmental mandates with costs that could not be determined. In 9 cases, CBO identified private-sector mandates in bills but could not determine whether the costs would exceed the threshold. (Tables 7 and 8 on pages 17 and 24 list all of the legislation containing mandates that CBO reviewed in 2014.)

	2010	2011	2012	2013	2014
	Intergovernmental Mandates				
Number of Statements Transmitted	474	434	428	437	539
Number of Statements That Identified Mandates	**64**	**56**	**68**	**39**	**47**
Mandate costs of the legislation would exceed the threshold	3	2	2	1	4
CBO could not determine whether mandate costs of the legislation would exceed the threshold	7	2	6	0	0
Mandate costs of the legislation would fall below the threshold	54	52	60	38	43
	Private-Sector Mandates				
Number of Statements Transmitted	474	434	428	437	539
Number of Statements That Identified Mandates	**85**	**67**	**80**	**53**	**75**
Mandate costs of the legislation would exceed the threshold	14	26	14	10	12
CBO could not determine whether mandate costs of the legislation would exceed the threshold	23	17	18	4	9
Mandate costs of the legislation would fall below the threshold	48	24	48	39	54

Source: Congressional Budget Office.

Notes: CBO also completed preliminary reviews and informal estimates for other legislation that are not included in this table.

The staff of the Joint Committee on Taxation examines tax provisions of legislation to identify federal mandates and estimates their costs. Such information is incorporated in CBO's mandate statements.

A mandate statement may cover more than one mandate; because the same mandate sometimes appears in multiple bills, a single mandate may be addressed in more than one CBO mandate statement.

Table 3.

Laws Enacted in 2014 That Contain Intergovernmental Mandates

Of the 224 laws enacted in 2014, 16 contain a total of 24 intergovernmental mandates. None of those laws include intergovernmental mandates with costs that the Congressional Budget Office estimates will exceed the statutory threshold ($76 million in 2014) established in the Unfunded Mandates Reform Act (UMRA). Only 13 laws containing intergovernmental mandates with costs estimated to exceed the statutory threshold have been enacted since UMRA became effective in 1996; those laws are listed in Appendix B.

Not all mandates are reviewed by CBO before enactment. In some cases, legislation is enacted without being considered by a committee. Some mandates are included in amendments made on the House or Senate floor or in conference after CBO's review. Others are included in appropriation bills, which UMRA does not direct CBO to review. Of the 24 intergovernmental mandates enacted in 2014, CBO reviewed all but 1 before enactment.

Public Law Number	Title of Legislation	Description of Mandate	Was the Mandate Reviewed by CBO Before Enactment?[a]
	Laws Containing Intergovernmental Mandates With Aggregate Costs That Exceed the Statutory Threshold		
		None	
	Laws Containing Intergovernmental Mandates With Aggregate Costs That Could Not Be Determined		
		None	
	Laws Containing Intergovernmental Mandates With Aggregate Costs That Fall Below the Statutory Threshold		
113-73	Joint resolution making further continuing appropriations for fiscal year 2014, and for other purposes	Extends until January 18, 2014, existing standards for the security of chemical facilities that require vulnerability assessments and for the development and implementation of site security plans	Yes
113-76	Consolidated Appropriations Act, 2014	Extends until October 4, 2014, existing standards for the security of chemical facilities that require vulnerability assessments and for the development and implementation of site security plans	Yes
113-121	Water Resources Reform and Development Act of 2014	Requires public entities to comply with watercraft inspections or other measures to prevent the spread of invasive species	Yes
113-164	Continuing Appropriations Resolution, 2015	Extends, through December 11, 2014, the Internet Tax Freedom Act, which prohibits some state and local governments from taxing Internet access	Yes
		Extends until December 11, 2014, existing standards for the security of chemical facilities that require vulnerability assessments and for the development and implementation of site security plans	Yes
113-175	Department of Veterans Affairs Expiring Authorities Act of 2014	Extends the period during which insurers have to cover certain care provided by the Department of Veterans Affairs to veterans with conditions related to military service	Yes

Continued

Table 3.   **Continued**

Laws Enacted in 2014 That Contain Intergovernmental Mandates

Public Law Number	Title of Legislation	Description of Mandate	Was the Mandate Reviewed by CBO Before Enactment?[a]
		Laws Containing Intergovernmental Mandates With Aggregate Costs That Fall Below the Statutory Threshold (Continued)	
113-179	Gun Lake Trust Land Reaffirmation Act	Extinguishes all rights to legal actions related to the land held in trust for the Match-E-Be-Nash-She-Wish Band of Pottawatomi Indians	Yes
113-183	Preventing Sex Trafficking and Strengthening Families Act	Increases the stringency of conditions in the implementation of state foster care programs	Yes
		Increases the stringency of conditions in the implementation of state child support enforcement programs by requiring states to implement electronic withholding of child support payments	No
113-200	STELA Reauthorization Act of 2014	Extends existing mandates on public entities that are copyright holders by extending, through December 31, 2019, the royalty rates that satellite carriers are required to pay for transmitting some copyrighted material	Yes
		Expands an existing mandate on low-power television stations (and other copyright holders) by allowing cable companies to retransmit signals from low-power stations to a broader audience area without paying royalties	Yes
113-202	Joint resolution making further continuing appropriations for fiscal year 2015, and for other purposes	Extends until December 13, 2014, existing standards for the security of chemical facilities that require vulnerability assessments and for the development and implementation of site security plans	Yes
		Extends, through December 13, 2014, the Internet Tax Freedom Act, which prohibits some state and local governments from taxing Internet access	Yes
113-203	Joint resolution making further continuing appropriations for fiscal year 2015, and for other purposes	Extends until December 17, 2014, existing standards for the security of chemical facilities that require vulnerability assessments and for the development and implementation of site security plans	Yes
		Extends, through December 17, 2014, the Internet Tax Freedom Act, which prohibits some state and local governments from taxing Internet access	Yes
113-232	Blackfoot River Land Exchange Act of 2014	Requires an exchange of land through federal statute, terminates rights to some parcels of land surrounding the Blackfoot River, and extinguishes some claims on those lands	Yes

Continued

Table 3. Continued

Laws Enacted in 2014 That Contain Intergovernmental Mandates

Public Law Number	Title of Legislation	Description of Mandate	Was the Mandate Reviewed by CBO Before Enactment?[a]
		Laws Containing Intergovernmental Mandates With Aggregate Costs That Fall Below the Statutory Threshold (Continued)	
113-235	Consolidated and Further Continuing Appropriations Act, 2015	Extends until September 30, 2015, existing standards for the security of chemical facilities that require vulnerability assessments and for the development and implementation of site security plans	Yes
		Extends, through November 1, 2015, the Internet Tax Freedom Act, which prohibits some state and local governments from taxing Internet access	Yes
113-254	Protecting and Securing Chemical Facilities From Terrorist Attacks Act of 2014	Modifies and extends for four years existing standards for the security of chemical facilities that require vulnerability assessments and for the development and implementation of site security plans	Yes
		Prohibits employers from discharging or discriminating against employees who report security problems at a covered chemical facility	Yes
113-286	Foreclosure Relief and Extension for Servicemembers Act of 2014	Extends the length of stay for civil proceedings related to real or personal property, mortgages, evictions, and foreclosures for service members whose military service has ended	Yes
113-290	Grand Portage Band per Capita Adjustment Act	Exempts some income of the members of the Grand Portage Band from state income tax	Yes
113-291	Carl Levin and Howard P. "Buck" McKeon National Defense Authorization Act for Fiscal Year 2015	Preempts state laws governing child custody if they are inconsistent with federal law or if they provide less protection for the rights of a parent who is a service member	Yes
		Preempts the authority of state and local governments to tax land and mineral interests taken into trust by the federal government for the Northern Cheyenne Tribe of Montana	Yes

Source: Congressional Budget Office.

Note: Under the Unfunded Mandates Reform Act, the staff of the Joint Committee on Taxation examines tax provisions of legislation to identify federal mandates and estimates their costs. Such information is incorporated in CBO's mandate statements.

a.   A response of "Yes" indicates that CBO reviewed legislation containing a version of the mandate prior to enactment, either in a cost estimate or a review of public laws during the current Congress.

Table 4.

Laws Enacted in 2014 That Contain Private-Sector Mandates

Of the 224 laws enacted last year, 26 contain one or more private-sector mandates, for a total of 55 such mandates enacted in 2014. Those laws contain a total of 5 mandates that the Congressional Budget Office estimated will impose costs on the private sector that exceed the annual threshold established in the Unfunded Mandates Reform Act ($152 million in 2014). Those 5 mandates are shown in the table in **bold type**. CBO has identified 141 private-sector mandates enacted since 1996 with costs estimated to exceed the annual threshold. Those mandates and the 97 public laws containing them are listed in Appendix B.

The laws enacted in 2014 also contain 3 private-sector mandates whose costs could not be determined; their costs may or may not be above the threshold. Those mandates are shown in the table in *italic type*. CBO estimated that the other 47 private-sector mandates enacted in 2014 will impose costs below the annual threshold. Those mandates are shown in regular type.

Not all mandates are reviewed by CBO before enactment. In some cases, legislation is enacted without being considered by a committee. Some mandates are included in amendments made on the House or Senate floor or in conference after CBO's review. Others are included in appropriation bills, which the Unfunded Mandates Reform Act does not direct CBO to review. Of the 55 private-sector mandates enacted in 2014, CBO reviewed 43 before enactment. Of the remaining 12 mandates not reviewed by CBO, 7 were enacted as provisions of appropriation acts. Most of the mandates not reviewed temporarily extended existing mandates, and none of those mandates is estimated to have a cost above the private-sector threshold.

Public Law Number	Title of Legislation	Description of Mandate	Was the Mandate Reviewed by CBO Before Enactment?[a]
		Laws Containing Private-Sector Mandates With Aggregate Costs That Exceed the Statutory Threshold	
113-76	Consolidated Appropriations Act, 2014	**Extends the authority of the Secretary of State to collect a surcharge on passport applications until September 30, 2014**	Yes
		Extends until October 4, 2014, existing standards for the security of chemical facilities that require vulnerability assessments and for the development and implementation of site security plans	No
		Extends until September 30, 2014, existing requirements for companies to safeguard and properly dispose of information collected from individuals who participate in the federal pre-screening program for air passengers	No
		Extends the restriction on sales of cluster munitions until September 30, 2014	No
113-159	Highway and Transportation Funding Act of 2014	**Extends customs user fees through fiscal year 2024**	Yes
113-175	Department of Veterans Affairs Expiring Authorities Act of 2014	**Extends the period during which insurers have to cover certain care provided by the Department of Veterans Affairs to veterans with conditions related to military service**	Yes

Continued

Table 4.   Continued

Laws Enacted in 2014 That Contain Private-Sector Mandates

Public Law Number	Title of Legislation	Description of Mandate	Was the Mandate Reviewed by CBO Before Enactment?[a]
		Laws Containing Private-Sector Mandates With Aggregate Costs That Exceed the Statutory Threshold (Continued)	
113-235	Consolidated and Further Continuing Appropriations Act, 2015	**Extends the authority of the Secretary of State to collect a surcharge on passport applications until September 30, 2015**	Yes
		Increases insurance premiums to be paid to the Pension Benefit Guaranty Corporation by sponsors of multiemployer defined-benefit pension plans	No
		Extends until February 27, 2015, existing requirements for companies to safeguard and properly dispose of information collected from individuals who participate in the federal pre-screening program for air passengers	Yes
		Extends the restriction on sales of cluster munitions until September 30, 2015	Yes
113-260	Designer Anabolic Steroid Control Act of 2014	**Regulates 25 new compounds and any compounds found to be structurally similar as anabolic steroids under the Controlled Substances Act**	Yes
		Requires any anabolic steroid or product containing an anabolic steroid to be labeled as such	Yes
		Laws Containing Private-Sector Mandates With Aggregate Costs That Could Not Be Determined	
113-144	Unlocking Consumer Choice and Wireless Competition Act	*Eliminates an existing right of action for wireless carriers (and others) who are currently able to pursue legal action against those who, without permission, circumvent the access controls on certain wireless telephone handsets sold after January 26, 2013*	Yes
113-179	Gun Lake Trust Land Reaffirmation Act	*Extinguishes all rights to legal actions related to the land held in trust for the Match-E-Be-Nash-She-Wish Band of Pottawatomi Indians*	Yes
113-272	Ukraine Freedom Support Act of 2014	*Prohibits private entities from engaging in certain transactions with sanctioned Russian entities*	Yes
		Laws Containing Private-Sector Mandates With Aggregate Costs That Fall Below the Statutory Threshold	
113-73	Joint resolution making further continuing appropriations for fiscal year 2014, and for other purposes	Extends the authority of the Secretary of State to collect a surcharge on passport applications until January 18, 2014	Yes

Continued

Table 4.   Continued

Laws Enacted in 2014 That Contain Private-Sector Mandates

Public Law Number	Title of Legislation	Description of Mandate	Was the Mandate Reviewed by CBO Before Enactment?[a]
		Laws Containing Private-Sector Mandates With Aggregate Costs That Fall Below the Statutory Threshold (Continued)	
113-73 (Continued)		Extends until January 18, 2014, existing standards for the security of chemical facilities that require vulnerability assessments and for the development and implementation of site security plans	No
		Extends until January 18, 2014, existing requirements for companies to safeguard and properly dispose of information collected from individuals who participate in the federal pre-screening program for air passengers	No
		Extends the restriction on sales of cluster munitions until January 18, 2014	No
113-79	Agricultural Act of 2014	Requires members of some agricultural industries to pay an assessment to fund federal research and promotion programs	Yes
		Requires country-of-origin labeling for venison	No
		Extends the authority of the National Oilheat Research Alliance to collect assessments from retail marketers and wholesale distributors of certain fuels	No
113-95	Support for the Sovereignty, Integrity, Democracy, and Economic Stability of Ukraine Act of 2014	Prohibits transactions with individuals subject to sanctions for actions and policies in Ukraine and with individuals in Russia	Yes
113-121	Water Resources Reform and Development Act of 2014	Requires private entities to comply with watercraft inspections or other measures to prevent the spread of invasive species	Yes
113-150	Sean and David Goldman International Child Abduction Prevention and Return Act of 2014	Prohibits transactions with people or entities associated with certain foreign countries by directing the President to take actions to persuade those countries to cooperate in cases involving international child abduction	Yes
113-160	An act to provide additional visas for the Afghan Special Immigrant Visa Program, and for other purposes	Increases the machine-readable visa fee or surcharge for nonimmigrant visas	No

Continued

Table 4. Continued

Laws Enacted in 2014 That Contain Private-Sector Mandates

Public Law Number	Title of Legislation	Description of Mandate	Was the Mandate Reviewed by CBO Before Enactment?[a]
		Laws Containing Private-Sector Mandates With Aggregate Costs That Fall Below the Statutory Threshold (Continued)	
113-164	Continuing Appropriations Resolution, 2015	Extends the authority of the Secretary of State to collect a surcharge on passport applications until December 11, 2014	Yes
		Extends until December 11, 2014, existing standards for the security of chemical facilities that require vulnerability assessments and for the development and implementation of site security plans	Yes
		Extends until December 11, 2014, existing requirements for companies to safeguard and properly dispose of information collected from individuals who participate in the federal pre-screening program for air passengers	Yes
		Extends the restriction on sales of cluster munitions until December 11, 2014	Yes
113-195	Sunscreen Innovation Act	Requires firms seeking to market certain new active ingredients in sunscreen to submit applications in a standardized format	Yes
113-200	STELA Reauthorization Act of 2014	Extends existing mandates on satellite carriers and copyright holders by extending, through December 31, 2019, the royalty rates that satellite carriers are required to pay for transmitting some copyrighted materials	Yes
		Expands an existing mandate on low-power television stations (and other copyright holders) by allowing cable companies to retransmit signals from low-power stations to a broader audience area without paying royalties	Yes
		Extends the prohibition that prevents television broadcasters from entering certain exclusive contracts with distributors of video programming services for the rights to carry (retransmit) their broadcast programs	Yes
		Extends the prohibition that prevents television broadcasters from receiving compensation from satellite carriers for retransmitting distant (nonlocal) broadcast programs to subscribers who live in areas that do not receive those broadcast signals	Yes

Continued

Table 4. *Continued*

Laws Enacted in 2014 That Contain Private-Sector Mandates

Public Law Number	Title of Legislation	Description of Mandate	Was the Mandate Reviewed by CBO Before Enactment?[a]
		Laws Containing Private-Sector Mandates With Aggregate Costs That Fall Below the Statutory Threshold (Continued)	
113-200 (Continued)		Prohibits television broadcasters from negotiating agreements on a joint basis with another television broadcaster in the same local market for retransmission of their broadcast programs by distributors of video programming services	Yes
		Requires satellite carriers to submit a report to the Federal Communications Commission containing certain information about the markets in which they provide local service	Yes
113-202	Joint resolution making further continuing appropriations for fiscal year	Extends the authority of the Secretary of State to collect a surcharge on passport applications until December 13, 2014	Yes
		Extends until December 13, 2014, existing standards for the security of chemical facilities that require vulnerability assessments and for the development and implementation of site security plans	Yes
		Extends until December 13, 2014, existing requirements for companies to safeguard and properly dispose of information collected from individuals who participate in the federal pre-screening program for air passengers	Yes
		Extends the restriction on sales of cluster munitions until December 13, 2014	Yes
113-203	Joint resolution making further continuing appropriations for fiscal year	Extends the authority of the Secretary of State to collect a surcharge on passport applications until December 17, 2014	Yes
		Extends until December 17, 2014, existing standards for the security of chemical facilities that require vulnerability assessments and the development and implementation of site security plans	Yes
		Extends until December 17, 2014, existing requirements for companies to safeguard and properly dispose of information collected from individuals who participate in the federal pre-screening program for air passengers	Yes
		Extends the restriction on sales of cluster munitions until December 17, 2014	Yes

Continued

Table 4.   Continued

Laws Enacted in 2014 That Contain Private-Sector Mandates

Public Law Number	Title of Legislation	Description of Mandate	Was the Mandate Reviewed by CBO Before Enactment?[a]
		Laws Containing Private-Sector Mandates With Aggregate Costs That Fall Below the Statutory Threshold (Continued)	
113-232	Blackfoot River Land Exchange Act of 2014	Requires an exchange of land through federal statute, terminates rights to some parcels of land surrounding the Blackfoot River, and extinguishes any past, present, or future claims on those lands	Yes
113-254	Protecting and Securing Chemical Facilities from Terrorist Attacks Act of 2014	Modifies and extends for four years existing standards for the security of chemical facilities that require vulnerability assessments and for the development and implementation of site security plans	Yes
		Prohibits employers from discharging or discriminating against employees who report security problems at a covered chemical facility	Yes
113-264	Federal Duck Stamp Act of 2014	Requires private entities to pay a higher annual fee for duck stamps, which serve as a federal permit that individuals are required to obtain to hunt migratory waterfowl	Yes
113-278	Venezuela Defense of Human Rights and Civil Society Act of 2014	Prohibits private entities from engaging in certain transactions with entities associated with human rights violations in Venezuela	Yes
		Revokes the visas of individuals found to be associated with human rights violations in Venezuela	Yes
113-281	Howard Coble Coast Guard and Maritime Transportation Act of 2014	Requires additional content in a vessel response plan prepared for a mobile offshore drilling unit	No
		Requires ship owners to pay certain expenses of seamen who are abandoned under certain conditions	No
113-286	Foreclosure Relief and Extension for Servicemembers Act of 2014	Extends the length of stay for civil proceedings related to real or personal property, mortgages, evictions, and foreclosures for service members whose military service has ended	Yes
113-291	Carl Levin and Howard P. "Buck" McKeon National Defense Authorization Act for Fiscal Year 2015	Requires private entities to file claims for losses covered by the Federal Aviation Administration's War Risk Insurance Program within two—or, in some cases, six—years of the loss	Yes

Source: Congressional Budget Office.

Notes: Under the Unfunded Mandates Reform Act, the staff of the Joint Committee on Taxation examines tax provisions of legislation to

Table 5.

Intergovernmental Mandates Reviewed by CBO in 2014 With Costs That Would Exceed the Statutory Threshold

In its review of legislation in 2014, the Congressional Budget Office identified three intergovernmental mandates with costs that would exceed the statutory threshold established in the Unfunded Mandates Reform Act ($76 million in 2014). One of those mandates, an increase in the minimum wage, appeared in two separate bills. Related bill numbers are given in parentheses.

Topic	Description of Mandate	Was a Version Enacted Into Law?
	Proposed Intergovernmental Mandates With Costs That Would Exceed the Statutory Threshold[a]	
Internet Taxation	Permanently prohibits all state and local governments from imposing taxes on Internet access (H.R. 3086)	No[a]
Minimum Wage	Requires employers whose workers are covered under the Fair Labor Standards Act to pay higher wages to some employees (S. 1737, S. 2223)	No
Postal Rates	Increases postal rates for first class mail, standard mail, and periodicals mailed through the Postal Service (S. 1486)	No

Source: Congressional Budget Office.

a. P.L. 113-164, P.L. 113-202, P.L. 113-203, and P.L. 113-235 each extended for brief periods of time the Internet Tax Freedom Act, which prohibits some state and local governments from taxing Internet access. H.R. 3086, as reviewed by CBO, would have prohibited all state and local governments from taxing Internet access and would have made the prohibition permanent.

Table 6.

Private-Sector Mandates Reviewed by CBO in 2014 With Costs That Would Exceed the Statutory Threshold or That Could Not Be Determined

In its review of legislation in 2014, the Congressional Budget Office identified 8 private-sector mandates in 12 different bills whose costs would exceed the statutory threshold established in the Unfunded Mandates Reform Act ($152 million in 2014). Four of those mandates were enacted. CBO identified another 9 private-sector mandates whose costs could not be determined. One of those 9 mandates was enacted.

Mandates with costs that would exceed the threshold or that could not be determined are listed below; related bill numbers are given in parentheses. In some cases, the same or similar private-sector mandate was identified in more than one bill (see Table 8 on page 24).

Topic	Description of Mandate	Was a Version Enacted Into Law?
	Proposed Private-Sector Mandates With Costs That Would Exceed the Statutory Threshold	
Chemicals	Requires owners and operators of certain chemical storage tanks to meet standards for tank construction, leak detection, spill prevention, lifecycle maintenance, and proof of financial responsibility; develop emergency response plans; and submit to periodic inspections (S. 1961)	No
Government Fees	Extends customs user fees (H.R. 5021, House Ways and Means; H.R. 5021, Senate Amendment 3582)	Yes (Public Law 113-159)[a]
Health Care	Extends the period during which insurers have to cover certain care provided by the Department of Veterans Affairs to veterans with conditions related to military service (H.R. 5404)	Yes (P.L. 113-175)[a]
Insurance	Requires policyholders of property and casualty insurance to pay higher surcharges in the event of a certified terrorist attack (H.R. 4871; S. 2244)	No
Minimum Wage	Requires employers whose workers are covered under the Fair Labor Standards Act to pay higher wages to some employees (S. 1737; S. 2223)	No
Pharmaceuticals	Regulates 25 new compounds and any compounds found to be structurally similar as anabolic steroids under the Controlled Substances Act (H.R. 4771, House Energy and Commerce; H.R. 4771, House Judiciary)	Yes (P.L. 113-260)[a]
Postal Rates	Increases postal rates for first class mail, standard mail, and periodicals mailed through the Postal Service (S. 1486)	No
Sanctions	Prohibits private entities from engaging in certain transactions with sanctioned Russian entities and from making significant investments in certain crude oil projects in Russia (S. 2828)	Yes (P.L. 113-272)[a,b]
	Proposed Private-Sector Mandates With Costs That Could Not Be Determined	
Automobile Safety	Requires manufacturers of motor vehicles to comply with regulations that establish the appropriate period for event data recorders to capture and record information (S. 1925)	No
Contracts	Prohibits contracts that contain binding arbitration clauses for resolving contractual disputes involving Servicemembers Civil Relief Act protections (S. 1593)	No

Continued

Table 6.   Continued

Private-Sector Mandates Reviewed by CBO in 2014 With Costs That Would Exceed the Statutory Threshold or That Could Not Be Determined

Topic	Description of Mandate	Was a Version Enacted Into Law?
	Proposed Private-Sector Mandates With Costs That Could Not Be Determined (Continued)	
Liability	Prohibits plaintiffs from filing a civil action against telecommunications providers for supplying the location of cell phones in emergency situations (H.R. 1575)	No
	Eliminates the ability of investors to sue to recover losses related to tick size (the increment by which the price of securities changes) by providing liability protection to issuers of securities that participate in a pilot program (H.R. 3448)	No
	Limits the contractual rights of companies by imposing a temporary stay on actions to terminate or modify contracts with large financial institutions that have entered bankruptcy for 48 hours after a bankruptcy petition is filed (H.R. 5421)	No
	Extinguishes all rights to legal actions related to the land held in trust for the Match-E-Be-Nash-She-Wish Band of Pottawatomi Indians (S. 1603, House Natural Resources; S. 1603, Senate Indian Affairs)	Yes (P.L. 113-179)[a]
	Terminates the ability of private entities to export items identified as foreign assistance to a country whose government is deposed by a coup or military action (S. 1857)	No
	Limits an existing right of action by extending civil and criminal liability protection to cybersecurity providers and other entities that share or use cyber threat information (S. 2588)	No
Trade	Prohibits the sale of defense articles and services to the government of Egypt under some circumstances (S. 1857)	No

Source: Congressional Budget Office.

Notes: The mandates in this table were identified by the Congressional Budget Office and the staff of the Joint Committee on Taxation (JCT) when a bill was reported by an authorizing committee or when CBO was asked to formally review a bill. In some cases, CBO issued more than one formal mandate statement for a topic. JCT examines the tax provisions of legislation to identify federal mandates and estimate their costs, and such information is incorporated into CBO's mandate statements.

a.   The full names of the public laws referred to in this table, ordered by law number, are as follows:
   • Public Law 113-159, the Highway and Transportation Funding Act of 2014
   • Public Law 113-175, the Department of Veterans Affairs Expiring Authorities Act of 2014
   • Public Law 113-179, the Gun Lake Trust Land Reaffirmation Act
   • Public Law 113-260, the Designer Anabolic Steroid Control Act of 2014
   • Public Law 113-272, the Ukraine Freedom Support Act of 2014

b.   During its review, CBO determined that the costs of the mandate in S. 2828 would exceed the annual threshold in the Unfunded Mandates Reform Act. The mandate was modified before enactment. CBO cannot determine whether the provision as enacted would exceed the annual threshold.

Table 7.

Bills Reviewed by CBO in 2014 That Contained Intergovernmental Mandates

Of the 539 bills that the Congressional Budget Office reviewed for mandates as defined in the Unfunded Mandates Reform Act (UMRA), 47 contained intergovernmental mandates. Of those 47 bills, 4 contained a mandate with costs that, in CBO's estimation, would exceed the statutory threshold established in UMRA ($76 million in 2014). Some bills were considered by more than one committee; in those cases, the table lists the various versions of that bill.

The bills containing intergovernmental mandates whose aggregate costs were estimated to exceed the statutory threshold are listed first in the table. Mandates whose costs would exceed the statutory threshold are in **bold type** and mandates with costs below the threshold are in regular type.

Bill Number (Committee or Status)	Title of Legislation	Description of Mandate
	Bills Containing Intergovernmental Mandates With Aggregate Costs That Exceed the Statutory Threshold[a]	
H.R. 3086	Permanent Internet Tax Freedom Act	**Permanently prohibits all state and local governments from imposing taxes on Internet access**
S. 1486	Postal Reform Act of 2014	**Increases postal rates for first class mail, standard mail, and periodicals mailed through the Postal Service**
S. 1737	Minimum Wage Fairness Act	**Requires employers whose workers are covered under the Fair Labor Standards Act to pay higher wages to some employees**
S. 2223	Minimum Wage Fairness Act	**Requires employers whose workers are covered under the Fair Labor Standards Act to pay higher wages to some employees**
	Bills Containing Intergovernmental Mandates With Aggregate Costs That Could Not Be Determined	
	None	
	Bills Containing Intergovernmental Mandates With Aggregate Costs That Fall Below the Statutory Threshold	
H.R. 1575	Kelsey Smith Act	Prohibits public entities from initiating civil or administrative proceedings against telecommunications providers that relay requested information and other assistance
H.R. 1771	North Korea Sanctions Enforcement Act of 2014	Prohibits public and private entities from exporting defense-related items, data, and services that are sent as nonhumanitarian assistance to countries that provide military equipment to North Korea
H.R. 2131	Supplying Knowledge-Based Immigrants and Lifting Levels of STEM Visas Act (SKILLS Visa Act)	Requires employers of some foreign workers to offer those workers the actual or prevailing wage paid to other workers of similar qualifications and experience
		Requires employers of some workers from Australia, Canada, Chile, Mexico, and Singapore to pay a fraud detection and prevention fee

Continued

Table 7. *Continued*

Bills Reviewed by CBO in 2014 That Contained Intergovernmental Mandates

Bill Number (Committee or Status)	Title of Legislation	Description of Mandate
	Bills Containing Intergovernmental Mandates With Aggregate Costs That Fall Below the Statutory Threshold (Continued)	
H.R. 2810	SGR Repeal and Medicare Beneficiary Access Act of 2013	Preempts state laws governing the evidentiary rules and practices of medical malpractice claims
H.R. 3361 (House Judiciary)	USA Freedom Act	Limits a right of action for public and private entities to sue in cases in which a defendant provides information to the federal government pursuant to a Foreign Intelligence Serveillance Act (FISA) order
		Requires public and private entities, when compelled to provide information about telephone calls to federal officials, to protect the secrecy of the records and to minimize any disruption of services
H.R. 3361 (House Permanent Select Committee on Intelligence)	USA Freedom Act	Limits a right of action for public and private entities to sue in cases in which a defendant provides information to the federal government pursuant to a FISA order
		Requires public and private entities, when compelled to provide information about telephone calls to federal officials, to protect the secrecy of the records and to minimize any disruption of services
H.R. 3448	Small Cap Liquidity Reform Act of 2013	Preempts state and local liability laws
		Eliminates the ability of investors to sue to recover losses related to tick size (the increment by which the price of securities changes) by providing liability protection to issuers of securities that participate in a pilot program
H.R. 3584	A bill to amend the Federal Home Loan Bank Act to authorize privately insured credit unions to become members of a federal home loan bank, and for other purposes	Preempts state laws that allow for voiding specific types of contracts between federal home loan banks and insolvent credit unions whose deposits are insured by private insurers
H.R. 3608	Grand Portage Band per Capita Adjustment Act	Exempts some income of members of the Grand Portage Band from state income tax
H.R. 4007 (House Homeland Security)	Chemical Facilities Anti-Terrorism Standards Program Authorization and Accountability Act of 2014	Makes permanent existing standards for the security of chemical facilities that require vulnerability assessments and for the development and implementation of site security plans
H.R. 4007 (Senate Homeland Security and Governmental Affairs)	Protecting and Securing Chemical Facilities From Terrorist Attacks Act	Extends existing standards for the security of chemical facilities that require vulnerability assessments and for the development and implementation of site security plans

Continued

Table 7.   Continued

Bills Reviewed by CBO in 2014 That Contained Intergovernmental Mandates

Bill Number (Committee or Status)	Title of Legislation	Description of Mandate
	Bills Containing Intergovernmental Mandates With Aggregate Costs That Fall Below the Statutory Threshold (Continued)	
H.R. 4007 (Senate Homeland Security and Governmental Affairs, Continued)		Prohibits employers from discharging or discriminating against employees who report security problems at a covered chemical facility
H.R. 4058	Preventing Sex Trafficking and Improving Opportunities for Youth in Foster Care Act	Increases the stringency of conditions in the implementation of state foster care programs
H.R. 4200	SBIC Advisers Relief Act of 2014	Prohibits state governments from requiring some advisers of small business investment companies to register, obtain licenses, and meet other requirements
H.R. 4350	Northern Cheyenne Lands Act	Preempts the authority of state and local governments to tax land and mineral interests taken into trust by the federal government for the Northern Cheyenne Tribe of Montana
H.R. 4435	Howard P. "Buck" McKeon National Defense Authorization Act for Fiscal Year 2015	Preempts state laws governing child custody if they are inconsistent with federal law or if they provide less protection for the rights of a parent who is a service member
H.R. 4554	Restricted Securities Relief Act of 2014	Prohibits states from requiring the registration or review of securities in some cases
H.R. 4565	Startup Capital Modernization Act of 2014	Prohibits states from requiring the registration or review of securities in some cases
H.R. 4871	TRIA Reform Act of 2014	Requires property and casualty insurers to offer terrorism insurance
		Requires insurers to administer surcharges on policyholders and remit the amounts collected to the federal government
		Requires policyholders of property and casualty insurance to pay higher surcharges in the event of a certified terrorist attack
		Requires property and casualty insurers to collect and report information about terrorism insurance policies
		Preempts some state laws that regulate insurance

Continued

Table 7. Continued

Bills Reviewed by CBO in 2014 That Contained Intergovernmental Mandates

Bill Number (Committee or Status)	Title of Legislation	Description of Mandate
	Bills Containing Intergovernmental Mandates With Aggregate Costs That Fall Below the Statutory Threshold (Continued)	
H.R. 4871 (Continued)		Requires producers that are members of the National Association of Registered Agents and Brokers to register with secretaries of state, meet state licensing requirements, complete education requirements, or be bonded
H.R. 5036	Satellite Television Access Reauthorization Act of 2014	Extends the royalty rates that satellite carriers are required to pay for transmitting some copyrighted materials
H.R. 5049	Blackfoot River Land Exchange Act	Requires an exchange of land through federal statute, terminates rights to some parcels of land surrounding the Blackfoot River, and extinguishes any past, present, or future claims on that land
H.R. 5404	Department of Veterans Affairs Expiring Authorities Act of 2014	Extends the period during which insurers have to cover certain care provided by the Department of Veterans Affairs to veterans with conditions related to military service
H.R. 5449	Passenger Rail Reform and Investment Act of 2014	Requires public entities to create plans for and submit reports about capital assets of intercity passenger rail systems
S. 42	Criminal Antitrust Anti-Retaliation Act of 2013	Prohibits employers from terminating or otherwise discriminating against employees who provided information or assisted in the investigation of a violation of federal antitrust law
S. 161	Little Shell Tribe of Chippewa Indians Restoration Act of 2013	Exempts some lands from taxation by state and local governments
S. 1217	Housing Finance Reform and Taxpayer Protection Act of 2014	Requires servicers of mortgages to provide information to the borrower about the mortgage within 15 days of receiving the contract
		Requires state banking agencies to notify federal regulators about the possible insolvency of an insured depository institution and its affiliates
		Requires the creditor of a junior mortgage lien or other credit lien that contains a loan-to-value ratio of 80 percent or more to notify the holder of the senior mortgage on the property within 30 days of when the junior lien has been approved

Continued

Table 7. Continued

Bills Reviewed by CBO in 2014 That Contained Intergovernmental Mandates

Bill Number (Committee or Status)	Title of Legislation	Description of Mandate
	Bills Containing Intergovernmental Mandates With Aggregate Costs That Fall Below the Statutory Threshold (Continued)	
S. 1217 (Continued)		Requires state insurance regulators to notify federal regulators if an approved private mortgage insurer is determined to be in a hazardous financial condition
		Preempts some state laws concerning insolvent guarantors and aggregators of loans
S. 1219	Pechanga Band of Luiseno Mission Indians Water Rights Settlement Act	Requires Pechanga Band of Luiseno Mission Indians to enact a tribal water code
S. 1448	Spokane Tribe of Indians of the Spokane Reservation Equitable Compensation Settlement Act	Extinguishes the monetary claims of the Spokane Tribe of Indians against the United States for hydropower revenues and for past and continued use of their land
S. 1451	Lake Tahoe Restoration Act of 2013	Requires owners and operators of watercraft to submit their watercraft for inspection and decontamination of invasive species prior to launching in waters of the Lake Tahoe Basin
S. 1474	Alaska Safe Families Act and Villages Act of 2014	Requires states to give full faith and credit to court orders and decrees issued by some Alaskan tribes
S. 1593	A bill to amend the Servicemembers Civil Relief Act to enhance the protections accorded to servicemembers and their spouses with respect to mortgages, and for other purposes	Requires public and private entities to comply with civil orders issued by the Attorney General to further investigations arising under the Servicemembers Civil Relief Act (SCRA)
		Expands limits on the ability of taxing authorities to require, without a court order, service members and their spouses who own businesses to sell property to pay tax liens
		Extends the length of stay of some civil proceedings
		Extends the length of time a service member is protected from a rescission or termination of a contract without a court order
		Prohibits contracts that contain binding arbitration clauses for resolving contractual disputes involving SCRA protections
		Prohibits penalties on prepayment of mortgage obligations by service members if penalties accrue during military service
		Prohibits public and private lending institutions from denying credit to service members on the basis of eligibility for SCRA protections

Continued

Table 7.   Continued

Bills Reviewed by CBO in 2014 That Contained Intergovernmental Mandates

Bill Number (Committee or Status)	Title of Legislation	Description of Mandate
Bills Containing Intergovernmental Mandates With Aggregate Costs That Fall Below the Statutory Threshold (Continued)		
S. 1593 (Continued)		Requires state or local licensing authorities to delay continuing education requirements of a service member to maintain a license for a trade or profession if such service member is receiving special pay for hostile fire or imminent danger
S. 1603 (House Natural Resources)	Gun Lake Trust Land Reaffirmation Act	Extinguishes all rights to legal actions related to the land held in trust for the Match-E-Be-Nash-She-Wish Band of Pottawatomi Indians
S. 1603 (Senate Indian Affairs)	Gun Lake Trust Land Reaffirmation Act	Extinguishes all rights to legal actions related to the land held in trust for the Match-E-Be-Nash-She-Wish Band of Pottawatomi Indians
S. 1857	Egypt Assistance Reform Act of 2013	Terminates the ability of public and private entities to export items identified as foreign assistance to a country whose government is deposed by a coup or military action
		Prohibits the sale of defense articles and services to the government of Egypt under some circumstances
S. 1870	Supporting At-Risk Children Act	Increases the stringency of conditions in foster care, adoption assistance, and child support enforcement programs
S. 1961	Chemical Safety and Drinking Water Protection Act of 2014	Requires owners and operators of certain chemical storage tanks to meet standards for tank construction, leak detection, spill prevention, life cycle maintenance, and proof of financial responsibility; develop emergency response plans; and submit to periodic inspections
S. 2040	Blackfoot River Land Exchange Act of 2014	Requires an exchange of land through federal statute, terminates rights to some parcels of land surrounding the Blackfoot River, and extinguishes any past, present, or future claims on that land
S. 2094	Vessel Incidental Discharge Act	Preempts state and local laws regulating ballast water and other discharges from vessels by establishing a national uniform standard and set of best practices
S. 2188	A bill to amend the Act of June 18, 1934, to reaffirm the authority of the Secretary of the Interior to take land into trust for Indian tribes	Expands an existing mandate that exempts land taken into trust for tribal individuals or tribal governments from state and local taxes
		Limits the ability of public and private entities to file legal claims related to trust lands of Indian tribes that were federally recognized after 1934

Continued

Table 7.   Continued

Bills Reviewed by CBO in 2014 That Contained Intergovernmental Mandates

Bill Number (Committee or Status)	Title of Legislation	Description of Mandate
	Bills Containing Intergovernmental Mandates With Aggregate Costs That Fall Below the Statutory Threshold (Continued)	
S. 2244	Terrorism Risk Insurance Program Reauthorization Act of 2014	Requires property and casualty insurers to offer terrorism insurance
		Requires insurers to administer surcharges on policyholders and remit the amounts collected to the federal government
		Requires policyholders of property and casualty insurance to pay higher surcharges in the event of a certified terrorist attack
		Preempts some state laws that regulate insurance
S. 2442	Northern Cheyenne Lands Act	Preempts the authority of state and local governments to tax land and mineral interests taken into trust by the federal government for the Northern Cheyenne Tribe of Montana
S. 2454	Satellite Television Access Reauthorization Act of 2014	Expands an existing mandate on low-power television stations (and other copyright holders) by allowing cable companies to retransmit signals from low-power stations to a broader audience area without paying royalties
		Extends the royalty rates that satellite carriers are required to pay for transmitting some copyrighted materials
S. 2588	Cybersecurity Information Sharing Act of 2014	Limits an existing right of action by extending civil and criminal liability protection to cybersecurity providers and other entities that share or use cyber threat information
		Preempts laws that require disclosure of shared cybersecurity information or records
		Preempts laws that restrict the cybersecurity monitoring, sharing, and countermeasure activities authorized by the bill
S. 2646	Runaway and Homeless Youth and Trafficking Prevention Act	Requires state and local law enforcement agencies to share and update more information on missing persons than required under current law

Source: Congressional Budget Office.

Note: The staff of the Joint Committee on Taxation examines tax provisions of legislation to identify federal mandates and to estimate their costs. Such information is incorporated in CBO's mandate statements.

a.   In certain cases, proposed legislation reviewed by CBO contained multiple mandates, some of which did not have costs exceeding the statutory threshold.

Table 8.

Bills Reviewed by CBO in 2014 That Contained Private-Sector Mandates

Of the 539 bills that the Congressional Budget Office reviewed for mandates as defined in the Unfunded Mandates Reform Act (UMRA), 75 contained private-sector mandates. Of those 75 bills, 12 contained mandates with costs that, in CBO's estimation, would exceed the statutory threshold established in UMRA—$152 million in 2014. For 9 of those 75 bills, CBO could not determine whether the aggregate cost of the mandates would exceed or fall below the statutory threshold. Some bills were considered by more than one committee or reviewed by CBO more than once; in those cases, the table lists the various versions of those bills.

Bills containing private-sector mandates whose aggregate costs are estimated to exceed the statutory threshold are listed first in the table. Mandates whose costs would exceed the statutory threshold are in **bold type**, mandates with uncertain costs are in *italic type*, and mandates with costs below the threshold are in regular type.

Bill Number (Committee or status)	Title of Legislation	Description of Mandate
Bills Containing Private-Sector Mandates With Aggregate Costs That Exceed the Statutory Threshold[a]		
H.R. 4771 (House Energy and Commerce)	Designer Anabolic Steroid Control Act of 2014	**Regulates 25 new compounds and any compounds found to be structurally similar as anabolic steroids under the Controlled Substances Act**
		Requires any anabolic steroid or product containing an anabolic steroid to be labeled as such
H.R. 4771 (House Judiciary)	Designer Anabolic Steroid Control Act of 2014	**Regulates 25 new compounds and any compounds found to be structurally similar as anabolic steroids under the Controlled Substances Act**
		Requires any anabolic steroid or product containing an anabolic steroid to be labeled as such
H.R. 4871	TRIA Reform Act of 2014	**Requires policyholders of property and casualty insurance to pay higher surcharges in the event of a certified terrorist attack**
		Requires property and casualty insurers to offer terrorism insurance
		Requires property and casualty insurers to collect and report information about terrorism insurance policies
		Requires insurers to administer surcharges on policyholders and remit the amounts collected to the federal government
H.R. 5021 (House Ways and Means)	Highway and Transportation Funding Act of 2014	**Extends customs user fees**
H.R. 5021 (Senate Amendment 3582)	Highway and Transportation Funding Act of 2014	**Extends the merchandise processing fee**

Continued

Table 8.

Bills Reviewed by CBO in 2014 That Contained Private-Sector Mandates

Bill Number (Committee or status)	Title of Legislation	Description of Mandate
	Bills Containing Private-Sector Mandates With Aggregate Costs That Exceed the Statutory Threshold[a] (Continued)	
H.R. 5404	Department of Veterans Affairs Expiring Authorities Act of 2014	Extends the period during which insurers have to cover certain care provided by the Department of Veterans Affairs to veterans with conditions related to military service
S. 1486	Postal Reform Act of 2014	Increases postal rates for first class mail, standard mail, and periodicals mailed through the Postal Service
		Requires national and state political committees to pay higher postal rates for third-class letters
		Requires postal annuitants enrolled in Postal Service health plans to enroll in Medicare if they are eligible and pay the associated premiums
S. 1737	Minimum Wage Fairness Act	Requires employers whose workers are covered under the Fair Labor Standards Act to pay higher wages to some employees
S. 1961	Chemical Safety and Drinking Water Protection Act of 2014	Requires owners and operators of certain chemical storage tanks to meet standards for tank construction, leak detection, spill prevention, life cycle maintenance, and proof of financial responsibility; develop emergency response plans; and submit to periodic inspections
S. 2223	Minimum Wage Fairness Act	Requires employers whose workers are covered under the Fair Labor Standards Act to pay higher wages to some employees
S. 2244	Terrorism Risk Insurance Program Reauthorization Act of 2014	Requires policyholders of property and casualty insurance to pay higher surcharges in the event of a certified terrorist attack
		Requires property and casualty insurers to offer terrorism insurance
		Requires insurers to administer surcharges on policyholders and remit the amounts collected to the federal government
S. 2828	Ukraine Freedom Support Act of 2014	Prohibits private entities from engaging in certain transactions with sanctioned Russian entities and from making significant investments in certain crude oil projects in Russia

Continued

Table 8.   **Continued**

Bills Reviewed by CBO in 2014 That Contained Private-Sector Mandates

Bill Number (Committee or status)	Title of Legislation	Description of Mandate
	Bills Containing Private-Sector Mandates With Aggregate Costs That Could Not Be Determined	
H.R. 1575	Kelsey Smith Act	*Prohibits plaintiffs from filing a civil action against telecommunications providers for supplying the location of cell phones in emergency situations*
		Requires telecommunications providers to share the location of cell phones in emergency situations without being presented with a warrant and without subjecting the request to internal criteria
H.R. 3448	Small Cap Liquidity Reform Act of 2013	*Eliminates the ability of investors to sue to recover losses related to tick size (the increment by which the price of securities changes) by providing liability protection to issuers of securities that participate in a pilot program*
		Requires companies in the pilot program related to tick size to notify the Securities and Exchange Commission if they elect not to participate
H.R. 5421	Financial Institution Bankruptcy Act of 2014	*Limits the contractual rights of companies by imposing a temporary stay on actions to terminate or modify contracts with large financial institutions that have entered bankruptcy for 48 hours after a bankruptcy petition is filed under the bankruptcy process established under the bill*
S. 1593	A bill to amend the Servicemembers Civil Relief Act to enhance the protections accorded to servicemembers and their spouses with respect to mortgages, and for other purposes	*Prohibits contracts that contain binding arbitration clauses for resolving contractual disputes involving Servicemembers Civil Relief Act (SCRA) protections*
		Prohibits lending institutions from denying credit to service members on the basis of eligibility for SCRA protection
		Extends the length of stay of some civil proceedings
		Prohibits penalties on prepayment of mortgage obligations by service members if the penalties accrue during military service
		Requires private entities to comply with civil orders issued by the Attorney General to further investigations arising under SCRA
		Extends the length of time a service member is protected from a rescission or termination of a contract without a court order

Continued

Table 8.   Continued

Bills Reviewed by CBO in 2014 That Contained Private-Sector Mandates

Bill Number (Committee or status)	Title of Legislation	Description of Mandate
	Bills Containing Private-Sector Mandates With Aggregate Costs That Could Not Be Determined (Continued)	
S. 1593 (Continued)		Increases the cost of an existing mandate on lenders by expanding the applicability of a cap on interest rates for certain student loans
		Prohibits residential lessors from imposing penalties for early termination of leases if the renter is a service member who moves into military housing
S. 1603 (House Natural Resources)	Gun Lake Trust Land Reaffirmation Act	*Extinguishes all rights to legal actions related to the land held in trust for the Match-E-Be-Nash-She-Wish Band of Pottawatomi Indians*
S. 1603 (Senate Indian Affairs)	Gun Lake Trust Land Reaffirmation Act	*Extinguishes all rights to legal actions related to the land held in trust for the Match-E-Be-Nash-She-Wish Band of Pottawatomi Indians*
S. 1857	Egypt Assistance Reform Act of 2013	*Terminates the ability of private entities to export items identified as foreign assistance to a country whose government is deposed by a coup or military action*
		Prohibits the sale of defense articles and services to the government of Egypt under some circumstances
S. 1925	Driver Privacy Act	*Requires manufacturers of motor vehicles to comply with regulations that establish the appropriate period for event data recorders to capture and record information*
S. 2588	Cyber Information Sharing Act of 2014	*Limits an existing right of action by extending civil and criminal liability protection to cybersecurity providers and other entities that share or use cyber threat information*
	Bills Containing Private-Sector Mandates With Aggregate Costs That Fall Below the Statutory Threshold	
H.R. 6	Domestic Prosperity and Global Freedom Act	Requires applicants for approval to export natural gas to publicly disclose the countries that would receive such exports
H.R. 1771	North Korea Sanctions Enforcement Act of 2014	Prohibits private entities from exporting defense-related items, data, and services that are sent as nonhumanitarian assistance to countries that provide military equipment to North Korea
		Revokes licenses for transactions that lack financial controls to ensure that such transactions will not facilitate the proliferation of weapons or human rights abuses by the North Korean government

Continued

Table 8.   Continued

Bills Reviewed by CBO in 2014 That Contained Private-Sector Mandates

Bill Number (Committee or status)	Title of Legislation	Description of Mandate
	Bills Containing Private-Sector Mandates With Aggregate Costs That Fall Below the Statutory Threshold (Continued)	
H.R. 1773	Agricultural Guestworker Act	Requires employers to deposit a portion of the wages of foreign agricultural workers into a federal trust fund
H.R. 2131	Supplying Knowledge-Based Immigrants and Lifting Levels of STEM Visas Act (SKILLS Visa Act)	Requires employers of some foreign workers to offer those workers the actual or prevailing wage paid to other workers of similar qualifications and experience
		Requires employers of some workers from Australia, Canada, Chile, Mexico, and Singapore to pay a fraud detection and prevention fee
H.R. 2673	Portfolio Lending and Mortgage Access Act	Limits an existing right of action against lenders by broadening the definition of mortgages that are granted legal protection from civil actions based on a claim that the lender failed to comply with ability-to-repay requirements
H.R. 2748	Postal Reform Act of 2013	Requires national and state political committees to pay higher postal rates for third-class letters
H.R. 2964	Public Access and Lands Improvement Act	Eliminates a right of action to seek judicial review of sales of salvageable timber on some federal lands affected by the 2013 Rim Fire in California
H.R. 3188	Rim Fire Emergency Salvage Act	Eliminates a right of action to seek judicial review of sales of salvageable timber on some federal lands affected by the 2013 Rim Fire in California
H.R. 3212	Sean and David Goldman International Child Abduction Prevention and Return Act of 2014	Prohibits private entities from engaging in transactions with sanctioned entities
H.R. 3361 (House Judiciary)	USA FREEDOM Act	Limits a right of action for private entities to sue in cases in which a defendant provides information to the federal government pursuant to a Foreign Intelligence Surveillance Act (FISA) order
		Requires private entities, when compelled to provide information about telephone calls to federal officials, to protect the secrecy of the records and to minimize any disruption of services
H.R. 3361 (House Permanent Select Committee on Intelligence)	USA FREEDOM Act	Limits a right of action for private entities to sue in cases in which a defendant provides information to the federal government pursuant to a FISA order
		Requires private entities, when compelled to provide information about telephone calls to federal officials, to protect the secrecy of the records and to minimize any disruption of services

Continued

Table 8.   Continued

Bills Reviewed by CBO in 2014 That Contained Private-Sector Mandates

Bill Number (Committee or status)	Title of Legislation	Description of Mandate
	Bills Containing Private-Sector Mandates With Aggregate Costs That Fall Below the Statutory Threshold (Continued)	
H.R. 3584	A bill to amend the Federal Home Loan Bank Act to authorize privately insured credit unions to become members of a federal home loan bank, and for other purposes	Requires insurers of credit union deposits to submit a copy of their annual audit to the National Credit Union Administration and to the Federal Housing Finance Agency for privately insured credit unions that are members of the Federal Home Loan Bank system
H.R. 3590	SHARE Act of 2013	Eliminates an individual's existing right to seek compensation from the federal government for damages occurring at a public target range supported by federal funds
H.R. 3675	Federal Communications Commission Process Reform Act of 2013	Requires commercial entities to pay higher regulatory fees to the Federal Communications Commission
H.R. 3676	Prohibiting In-Flight Voice Communications on Mobile Wireless Devices Act of 2013	Prohibits airline passengers from making voice calls during a domestic flight
H.R. 4007 (House Homeland Security)	Chemical Facilities Anti-Terrorism Standards Program Authorization and Accountability Act of 2014	Makes permanent existing standards for the security of chemical facilities that require vulnerability assessments and for the development and implementation of site security plans
H.R. 4007 (Senate Homeland Security and Governmental Affairs)	Protecting and Securing Chemical Facilities From Terrorist Attacks Act of 2014	Extends existing standards for the security of chemical facilities that require vulnerability assessments and for the development and implementation of site security plans
		Prohibits employers from discharging or discriminating against employees who report security problems at a covered chemical facility
H.R. 4250	Sunscreen Innovation Act	Requires firms seeking to market certain new active ingredients in sunscreen to submit applications in a standardized format
H.R. 4321	Employee Privacy Protection Act	Requires employers to obtain in writing their employees' preferred method of being contacted by union representatives
H.R. 4411	Hezbollah International Financing Prevention Act of 2014	Prohibits financial institutions from opening or maintaining certain types of financial accounts for entities that are knowingly affiliated with Hezbollah
H.R. 4435	Howard P. "Buck" McKeon National Defense Authorization Act for Fiscal Year 2015	Requires private entities to file claims for losses covered by the Federal Aviation Administration's War Risk Insurance Program within two—or, in some cases, six—years of the loss

Continued

Table 8.   Continued

Bills Reviewed by CBO in 2014 That Contained Private-Sector Mandates

Bill Number (Committee or status)	Title of Legislation	Description of Mandate
	Bills Containing Private-Sector Mandates With Aggregate Costs That Fall Below the Statutory Threshold (Continued)	
H.R. 4466	Financial Regulatory Clarity Act of 2014	Requires private entities to pay higher regulatory fees to the Securities and Exchange Commission
H.R. 4568	Small Business Freedom to Grow Act of 2014	Requires private entities to pay higher regulatory fees to the Securities and Exchange Commission
H.R. 4569	Disclosure Modernization and Simplification Act of 2014	Requires private entities to pay higher regulatory fees to the Securities and Exchange Commission
H.R. 4570	Private Placement Improvement Act of 2014	Requires private entities to pay higher regulatory fees to the Securities and Exchange Commission
H.R. 4572	STELA Reauthorization Act of 2014	Extends the prohibition that prevents television broadcasters from entering certain exclusive contracts with distributors of video programming services for the rights to carry (retransmit) their broadcast programs
		Extends the prohibition that prevents television broadcasters from receiving compensation from satellite carriers for retransmitting distant (nonlocal) broadcast programs to subscribers who live in areas that do not receive those broadcast signals
		Prohibits television broadcasters from negotiating agreements on a joint basis with another television broadcaster in the same local market for retransmission of their broadcast programs by distributors of video programming services
		Requires satellite carriers to submit a report to the Federal Communications Commission containing certain information about the markets in which they provide local service
H.R. 4587	Venezuelan Human Rights and Democracy Protection Act	Prohibits private entities from engaging in certain transactions with entities associated with human rights violations in Venezuela
		Revokes the visas of individuals found to be associated with human rights violations in Venezuela
H.R. 4697	Small-Cap Access to Capital Act	Requires some emerging growth companies to comply with additional requirements (mostly by providing additional information) when registering securities with the Securities and Exchange Commission
H.R. 5036	Satellite Television Access Reauthorization Act of 2014	Extends existing mandates on satellite carriers and copyright holders by extending the royalty rates that satellite carriers are required to pay for transmitting some copyrighted materials

Continued

Table 8.   **Continued**

Bills Reviewed by CBO in 2014 That Contained Private-Sector Mandates

Bill Number (Committee or status)	Title of Legislation	Description of Mandate
	Bills Containing Private-Sector Mandates With Aggregate Costs That Fall Below the Statutory Threshold (Continued)	
H.R. 5049	Blackfoot River Land Exchange Act of 2014	Requires an exchange of land through federal statute, terminates rights to some parcels of land surrounding the Blackfoot River, and extinguishes any past, present, or future claims on that land
H.R. 5069	Federal Duck Stamp Act of 2014	Requires private entities to pay a higher annual fee for duck stamps, which serve as a federal permit that individuals are required to obtain to hunt migratory waterfowl
H.R. 5094	A bill to amend title 38, United States Code, to authorize the Secretary of Veterans Affairs to recoup certain bonuses or awards paid to employees of the Department of Veterans Affairs, and for other purposes	Requires employees of the Department of Veterans Affairs to repay all or a portion of the amount paid as awards or bonuses if directed by the Secretary of Veterans Affairs
H.R. 5449	Passenger Rail Reform and Investment Act of 2014	Requires Amtrak to create plans for and submit reports about the capital assets of intercity passenger rail systems
		Requires the Amtrak Board of Directors to consider options to improve boarding procedures and to evaluate requests to use an Amtrak right-of-way for other business activities
		Requires Amtrak to establish certain financial controls and submit to the Congress various reports, including a report on options to enhance development around Amtrak stations
		Modifies Amtrak's role on some rail advisory committees
S. 42	Criminal Antitrust Anti-Retaliation Act of 2013	Prohibits employers from terminating or otherwise discriminating against employees who provided information or assisted in the investigation of a violation of federal antitrust law
S. 429	Concrete Masonry Products Research, Education, and Promotion Act of 2013	Requires manufacturers of concrete masonry products, such as cinder blocks and concrete pavers, to pay an assessment
S. 517	Unlocking Consumer Choice and Wireless Competition Act	Eliminates an existing right of action for wireless carriers (and others) who are currently able to pursue legal action against those who, without permission, circumvent the access controls on certain wireless telephone handsets sold after January 26, 2013

Continued

Table 8.   Continued

Bills Reviewed by CBO in 2014 That Contained Private-Sector Mandates

Bill Number (Committee or status)	Title of Legislation	Description of Mandate
	Bills Containing Private-Sector Mandates With Aggregate Costs That Fall Below the Statutory Threshold (Continued)	
S. 1217	Housing Finance Reform and Taxpayer Protection Act of 2014	Requires servicers of mortgages to provide information to the borrower about the mortgage within 15 days of receiving the contract
		Requires the creditor of a junior mortgage lien or other credit lien that contains a loan-to-value ratio of 80 percent or more to notify the holder of the senior mortgage on the property within 30 days of when the junior lien has been approved
S. 1406	Prevent All Soring Tactics Act of 2014	Prohibits the use of any device placed on a horse's limb to artificially alter its gait (known as an action device)
S. 1451	Lake Tahoe Restoration Act of 2013	Requires owners and operators of watercraft to submit their watercraft for inspection and decontamination of invasive species prior to launching in waters of the Lake Tahoe Basin
S. 1463	Captive Primate Safety Act	Prohibits any person from importing, exporting, transporting, selling, receiving, acquiring, or purchasing nonhuman primates in interstate or foreign commerce
S. 1474	Alaska Safe Families and Villages Act of 2014	Eliminates an existing right of action against the State of Alaska
S. 1865	Migratory Bird Habitat Investment and Enhancement Act	Requires private entities to pay a higher annual fee for duck stamps, which serve as a federal permit that individuals are required to obtain to hunt migratory waterfowl
S. 1898	Truth in Settlements Act of 2014	Requires some issuers of securities to describe in reports to the Securities and Exchange Commission any tax deduction claimed that relates to payments required under a covered settlement agreement with a federal agency
S. 1933	Global Magnitsky Human Rights Accountability Act	Prohibits transactions related to any property or interests in property belonging to individuals associated with violations of human rights in foreign countries
		Revokes the visas of individuals found to be associated with violations of human rights in foreign countries
S. 2040	Blackfoot River Land Exchange Act of 2014	Requires an exchange of land through federal statute, terminates rights to some parcels of land surrounding the Blackfoot River, and extinguishes any past, present, or future claims on that land

Continued

Table 8. Continued

Bills Reviewed by CBO in 2014 That Contained Private-Sector Mandates

Bill Number (Committee or status)	Title of Legislation	Description of Mandate
	Bills Containing Private-Sector Mandates With Aggregate Costs That Fall Below the Statutory Threshold (Continued)	
S. 2094	Vessel Incidental Discharge Act	Prohibits manufacturers and importers of water treatment technology from selling such technology unless it has been certified by the United States Coast Guard or certified by a foreign entity and deemed to meet equivalent levels of performance and safety
S. 2124	Support for the Sovereignty, Integrity, Democracy, and Economic Stability of Ukraine Act of 2014	Prohibits transactions with individuals subject to sanctions for actions and policies in Ukraine and with individuals in Russia
S. 2141	Sunscreen Innovation Act	Requires firms seeking to market certain new active ingredients in sunscreen to submit applications in a standardized format
S. 2142	Venezuela Defense of Human Rights and Civil Society Act of 2014	Prohibits transactions related to any property or interests in property belonging to individuals associated with human rights violations in Venezuela
		Revokes visas of individuals found to be associated with human rights violations in Venezuela
S. 2188	A bill to amend the Act of June 18, 1934, to reaffirm the authority of the Secretary of the Interior to take land into trust for Indian tribes	Limits the ability of private entities to file legal claims related to trust lands of Indian tribes that were federally recognized after 1934
S. 2454	Satellite Television Access Reauthorization Act of 2014	Extends existing mandates on satellite carriers and copyright holders by extending the royalty rates that satellite carriers are required to pay for transmitting some copyrighted materials
		Expands an existing mandate on low-power television stations (and other copyright holders) by allowing cable companies to retransmit signals from low-power stations to a broader audience area without paying royalties
S. 2581	Child Nicotine Poisoning Prevention Act of 2014	Requires manufacturers of consumer products containing liquid nicotine to use special packaging for such products to make them child resistant
S. 2940	Presidential Library Donation Reform Act of 2014	Requires organizations established for the purpose of raising funds for Presidential libraries or their related facilities to submit information to the National Archives and Records Administration

Continued

Table 8. Continued

Bills Reviewed by CBO in 2014 That Contained Private-Sector Mandates

Bill Number (Committee or status)	Title of Legislation	Description of Mandate
	Bills Containing Private-Sector Mandates With Aggregate Costs That Fall Below the Statutory Threshold (Continued)	
S. 2799	Satellite Television Access and Viewer Rights Act	Extends the prohibition that prevents television broadcasters from entering certain exclusive contracts with distributors of video programming services for the rights to carry (retransmit) their broadcast programs
		Extends the prohibition that prevents television broadcasters from receiving compensation from satellite carriers for retransmitting distant (nonlocal) broadcast programs to subscribers who live in areas that do not receive those broadcast signals
		Extends the requirement on broadcasters, cable operators, and satellite carriers to negotiate retransmission agreements in good faith
		Prohibits television broadcasters from negotiating agreements on a joint basis with another television broadcaster in the same local market for retransmission of their broadcast programs by distributors of video programming services
		Prohibits local broadcasters from using retransmission agreements to limit the ability of cable operators or satellite carriers to retransmit other broadcast signals they are authorized to carry

Source: Congressional Budget Office.

Note: The staff of the Joint Committee on Taxation examines tax provisions of legislation to identify federal mandates and estimate their costs. Such information is incorporated into CBO's mandate statements.

a. In certain cases, proposed legislation reviewed by CBO contained multiple mandates, some of which did not have costs exceeding the statutory threshold

Appendix A:
Overview of Key Provisions in the Unfunded Mandates Reform Act

The Unfunded Mandates Reform Act of 1995 (UMRA) comprises four titles that address how various parts of the federal government should handle proposed and existing mandates imposed on state, local, and tribal governments and on the private sector.

■ Title I, Legislative Accountability and Reform, requires the Congressional Budget Office and authorizing committees that oversee federal programs and authorize appropriations to develop and report information about the existence and costs of mandates in proposed legislation.[1] It also establishes mechanisms for bringing that information to the attention of the Congress before such legislation is considered on the floor of the House or Senate.

■ Title II, Regulatory Accountability and Reform, applies to actions of federal agencies in implementing federal law. It requires most agencies in the executive branch (except some independent regulatory agencies) to assess the effects of their regulatory actions on state, local, and tribal governments and on the private sector. It also requires that statements about such effects accompany certain significant regulations, that agencies seek input from other levels of government in developing regulations, and that agencies consider alternatives that would ease the financial burden of regulations.

■ Title III, Review of Federal Mandates, required the now defunct Advisory Commission on Intergovernmental Relations (ACIR) to prepare three reports: a baseline study of the costs and benefits of federal mandates imposed on state, local, and tribal governments; a review of the impact of unfunded federal mandates on those governments along with recommendations for easing, consolidating, or terminating mandates; and an annual report identifying federal court rulings that required state, local, or tribal governments to undertake additional responsibilities and activities.[2]

■ Title IV, Judicial Review, allows for limited judicial review of certain actions by agencies and of rules developed under title II of UMRA.

This appendix focuses on title I, which prescribes CBO's responsibilities under the act.

Defining Mandates

Under UMRA, a mandate is any provision in legislation, statute, or regulation that would impose an enforceable duty on state, local, or tribal governments or the private sector or that would reduce or eliminate the amount of funding authorized to cover the direct costs of existing mandates. UMRA does not define "enforceable duty," but CBO has interpreted the term to mean actions that

---

1. Authorizing committees have legislative jurisdiction over the establishment, operation, and continuation of federal programs or agencies; they also control spending for programs other than those that receive annual appropriations under the aegis of the appropriations committees.

2. ACIR completed and released the report on judicial mandates in July 1995. In January 1996, the commission published a preliminary report on the impact of federal mandates imposed on state and local governments. ACIR received no appropriations after fiscal year 1996 and was terminated at the end of that year.

would be either required or prohibited by the sovereign authority of the United States. For instance, a provision that would require companies to comply with a federal safety or environmental standard—or that would prohibit a business activity or establish a mandatory fee for businesses—would impose a mandate. In addition, for some large entitlement programs—those that provide $500 million or more annually to state, local, or tribal governments—a new condition on, or a reduction in, federal assistance would be a mandate, but only if those governments lack the flexibility to offset the new costs or the loss of federal funding with reductions elsewhere in the program.

A duty that arises out of participation in a voluntary federal program or that is a condition for receiving federal assistance does not fall within UMRA's definition of a mandate because such a duty is not compulsory. Some federal programs may establish requirements for participants that, by UMRA's definition, are not considered mandates even though the participants might incur significant costs as a result of the requirements. Nevertheless, CBO identifies those costs whenever possible. For example, the Clean Estuaries Act of 2014 (as ordered reported by the Senate Committee on Environment and Public Works in April 2014) would have added new requirements for states that participate in the National Estuaries Program (NEP). To participate in the program, states must submit comprehensive conservation and management plans, and the bill would have added provisions regarding planning, monitoring, and educational activities. States' participation in NEP, however, is voluntary, and states could choose not to participate in NEP and therefore not comply with the program's new requirements. Hence, under the guidelines specified by UMRA, those provisions of the bill contained no intergovernmental mandates.

Estimating the Costs of Mandates

Direct costs of mandates are defined in UMRA as amounts that the private sector or state, local, or tribal governments would be required to spend to comply with the enforceable duty, including amounts that states, localities, or tribes would be prohibited from raising in revenues. Additionally, when the mandate takes the form of a restriction on the ability of a private-sector entity to generate revenue, CBO measures the cost of that mandate as the direct loss of income. Such losses are not explicitly included in UMRA's definition of costs, but

CBO interprets UMRA's definition of a mandate to include not only requirements that would result in expenditures but also prohibitions that would result in lost income. Thus, in cases in which legislation would ban the production or sale of a good, CBO would measure the cost of the mandate as the net income forgone because of the ban. For example, CBO's estimate for the Synthetic Drug Control Act of 2011 included forgone income from lost sales in the estimated cost of a ban on certain synthetic chemicals.

CBO estimates direct costs as the total cost incurred by the entities on which the mandate is imposed, regardless of whether those costs may be passed on to other entities, such as consumers and workers. Direct costs exclude amounts that public or private entities would spend to comply with applicable laws, regulations, or professional standards in effect when the federal mandate is adopted. As directed by UMRA, CBO assumes that public and private entities would comply with mandates as efficiently as possible. Moreover, such costs are limited to spending that would result directly from the enforceable duty imposed by the legislation rather than from the legislation's broad effects on the economy. Therefore, estimates of mandate costs do not include the effects of each bill on gross domestic product, employment, or inflation.[3]

In addition, in CBO's estimates, direct costs are offset by any direct savings that would result from complying with the mandate or by savings from other provisions of the same legislation that govern the same activity as the one affected by the mandate. Direct savings do not include the impact of any authorization of appropriations in the same bill, or any funding authorized under current law, that might be used to help pay for a mandate.

Because the term "mandate" is defined narrowly in UMRA, the budgetary effects that legislation may have on other governments or the private sector are not solely the result of mandates. For example, costs associated with complying with conditions of receiving grants for most new or existing programs are not considered mandate costs under UMRA. Most of the nonmandate costs to governments or the private sector that CBO identifies

---

3. For more information about estimating the costs of mandates on the private sector, see Congressional Budget Office, *Private-Sector Mandates in Federal Legislation* (January 2013), www.cbo.gov/publication/43840.

when reviewing bills would result from conditions for receiving federal aid or participating in voluntary federal programs.

CBO's Role in Preparing Mandate Cost Statements

UMRA requires CBO to prepare mandate statements for bills that are approved by authorizing committees. In those statements, CBO must specify whether the direct costs of mandates in a bill would exceed the statutory threshold established under UMRA. If the total direct costs of all mandates in the bill are above the threshold in any of the first five fiscal years in which the mandates are effective, CBO must provide an estimate of those costs (if feasible) and explain the basis of the estimate.[4] In some cases, CBO cannot estimate the cost of a mandate—for instance, when much of its impact would depend on the nature of the implementing regulations that would be issued by federal agencies. If CBO cannot estimate the cost of a mandate, it must explain why such an estimate is not feasible. The mandate statement that CBO prepares also must include an assessment of whether the bill authorizes or otherwise provides funding to cover the costs of any new federal mandate. In the case of intergovernmental mandates, the cost statement must, under certain circumstances, include an estimate of the appropriations needed to fund such authorizations for up to 10 years after the mandate takes effect.

UMRA also requires Congressional committees to report information about the existence and costs of mandates in proposed legislation. Authorizing committees must publish CBO's mandate statements in their reports or in the *Congressional Record* before a bill is considered on the floor of the House or the Senate.

The Congress may also call on CBO to prepare analyses of federal mandates at other stages of the legislative process. At the request of a Senator, CBO must estimate the costs of intergovernmental mandates contained in an amendment the Senator may wish to offer. At the request of the Chairman or Ranking Member of a committee, CBO will help analyze the impact of proposed legislation,

conduct special studies of legislative proposals, or compare a federal agency's estimate of the costs of proposed regulations to implement a federal mandate with CBO's estimate.

Because UMRA requires CBO to issue mandate statements when bills are approved by authorizing committees, not all legislative provisions are reviewed for mandates. For example, a mandate statement might not be available when legislation is considered by the House or Senate without prior approval by a committee; when a bill is amended on the floor or in conference to include a provision that contains a mandate; or, in some cases, when a mandate is included in an appropriation bill. Still, UMRA requires conference committees to ensure, "to the greatest extent practicable," that CBO prepares statements for conference agreements or amended bills if they contain mandates not previously considered by either the House or the Senate or if they impose direct costs that are greater than those in a version considered earlier.

Additionally, not all legislation is subject to UMRA's requirements. In enacting the law, the Congress recognized that instances might arise in which budgetary considerations—such as who would bear the costs that a law might impose—should not be a key part of the debate about a piece of legislation. Therefore, UMRA excludes from its procedures provisions that deal with constitutional or statutory rights, implement international treaty obligations, are necessary for national security, or alter provisions of the Social Security Act related to old-age, survivors', or disability benefits.

Enforcement Mechanisms

UMRA sets out rules for both the House and the Senate that prohibit either chamber from considering legislation unless certain conditions are met. Specifically, UMRA prohibits the consideration of a reported bill unless the committee has published a statement from CBO about the costs of intergovernmental or private-sector mandates.

The rules preclude consideration of reported legislation that contains intergovernmental mandates with direct costs above the statutory threshold unless the legislation provides direct spending authority or authorizes appropriations sufficient to cover those costs. An authorization of an appropriation will not be sufficient unless the authorized amounts are specified for each year (up to

---

4. The statutory thresholds are $50 million for intergovernmental mandates and $100 million for private-sector mandates in 1996 dollars, adjusted annually for inflation. (The thresholds in 2014 were $76 million for intergovernmental mandates and $152 million for private-sector mandates.)

10 years) after the effective date and the legislation provides a way to terminate or scale back the mandate if the federal agency determines that the appropriated funds are not sufficient to cover those costs.

UMRA does not expressly require CBO to prepare mandate statements for appropriation bills. In general, UMRA's points of order do not apply to the provisions of bills or resolutions reported by the appropriations committees (except legislative provisions). However, legislative provisions in such bills—or amendments to them—that would increase the direct costs of intergovernmental mandates are not in order for consideration on the House or Senate floor unless an appropriate CBO statement is provided.[5]

The rules are not automatically enforced, however; a Member must raise a point of order to enforce them. (A point of order is an objection raised by a Member on the floor of the House or Senate that questions an action being taken as contrary to the rules of that body.) If a point of order is raised in the House or Senate as provided for in UMRA, each chamber resolves the issue according to its established rules and procedures.

---

5. In many cases, it is not clear what constitutes a legislative provision in an appropriation bill. Therefore, CBO prepares mandate statements for those bills only when requested. On an informal basis, however, CBO reviews all appropriation bills as they move through the legislative process and alerts the appropriation clerks if it identifies any intergovernmental mandates.

Appendix B:
Mandates Enacted Between
1996 and 2014 With Estimated Costs That
Exceed the Statutory Threshold

This appendix lists the intergovernmental (Table B-1) and private-sector (Table B-2) mandates enacted from 1996 through 2014 that the Congressional Budget Office has identified as imposing costs above the annual thresholds established in the Unfunded Mandates Reform Act. From 1996 through 2014, CBO has identified intergovernmental mandates with costs that exceed the annual threshold in less than 1 percent of public laws, and private-sector mandates with such costs in less than 5 percent of the laws enacted.

Table B-1.

Enacted Intergovernmental Mandates With Estimated Costs That Exceed the Statutory Threshold, 1996 to 2014

From 1996 through 2014, 13 laws have been enacted that contained a total of 18 intergovernmental mandates with costs that exceeded the threshold established in the Unfunded Mandates Reform Act. In 1996, the threshold for intergovernmental mandates was $50 million. That amount has been adjusted annually for inflation, and in 2014 the threshold was $76 million.

No laws enacted in 2014 contained intergovernmental mandates with costs above the threshold; the last such laws were enacted in 2010.

Topic	Description of Mandate	Public Law Number
Child Nutrition	Requires schools to provide meals that comply with new standards for menu planning and nutrition	111-296
	Requires schools to comply with nutrition standards for all food sold in schools	111-296
Child Support	Eliminates matching federal payments for some spending on child support	109-171
Driver's Licenses, Identification Cards, and Vital Statistics Documents	Requires state and local governments to meet certain standards for issuing driver's licenses, identification cards, and vital statistics documents	108-458
Food Stamp Administration	Reduces federal funding for administering the Food Stamp program (now the Supplemental Nutrition Assistance Program)	105-185
Health Care	Imposes notice and reporting requirements on health insurance plans (including self-insured plans), employers, and other public and private entities	111-148
	Requires health insurance plans (including self-insured plans) to comply with new standards for extending coverage to beneficiaries and their dependents	111-148
	Requires public and private employers to pay an excise tax on employer-sponsored health insurance coverage defined as having high costs	111-148
	Requires health insurance plans (including self-insured plans) to pay an annual fee based on the average number of people covered by the policy	111-148
	Requires public and private entities that handle health information to comply with new regulations	111-148
Internet Taxation	Temporarily preempts states' authority to tax certain Internet services and transactions	108-435
	Extends the preemption contained in Public Law 108-435 of states' authority to tax certain Internet services and transactions through most of 2011	110-108
Minimum Wage	Increases the minimum wage paid by state and local governments to their employees	104-188, 110-28
Premium Taxes on Prescription Drug Plans	Preempts state taxes on premiums for certain prescription drug plans	108-173
Rail and Transit	Requires all public transit and rail carriers to train workers and submit reports to the Department of Homeland Security	110-53
	Requires commuter railroads to install train control technology	110-432
Tax Withholding	Requires state and local governments to withhold taxes on certain payments for property and services	109-222

Table B-2.

Enacted Private-Sector Mandates With Estimated Costs That Exceed the Statutory Threshold, 1996 to 2014

From 1996 through 2014, the Congressional Budget Office identified 141 private-sector mandates in 97 public laws with costs estimated to exceed the annual threshold. In 1996, the threshold established in the Unfunded Mandates Reform Act (UMRA) for private-sector mandates was $100 million. That amount has been adjusted annually for inflation; in 2014, the threshold was $152 million.

CBO has identified private-sector mandates with costs estimated to exceed the threshold in less than 5 percent of the laws enacted since UMRA became effective in 1996. Over half of those mandates involve taxes or government fees. Many of the mandates temporarily extended existing mandates for a period of time.

Topic	Description of Mandate	Public Law Number[a]
Agriculture	Changes the method by which minimum prices are established for fluid milk in different regions of the country	106-113
	Requires country-of-origin labels for various foods	107-171, 110-246
Aviation	Imposes security procedures and user fees to fund aviation security programs	107-71, 113-67
	Requires owners of aircraft operating in congested airspace or at congested airports to install new communications equipment	112-95
	Prohibits the operation of certain aircraft that are not in compliance with low-noise standards	112-95
Bankruptcy	Changes procedures for administering bankruptcy claims	109-8
Campaign Finance Reform	Changes procedures for the collection and use of campaign contributions	107-155
Coal Mines	Imposes mining reclamation fees on operators of coal mines	109-54, 109-234, 109-432
	Requires operators of underground coal mines to install equipment to improve accident preparedness	109-236
Conflict Minerals	Requires manufacturers that use certain minerals to disclose where they obtained such minerals and to take measures to verify whether using such minerals benefits any armed groups in the Democratic Republic of Congo or an adjoining country	111-203
Consumer Product Safety	Requires manufacturers, distributors, retailers, and importers of consumer products to abide by new standards and labeling requirements	110-314
Elimination of Right to Seek Compensation	Limits possible recoveries on terrorism-related lawsuits against Libya	110-301
Energy	Requires motor vehicle fuel to contain a certain volume of fuel from a renewable source	109-58, 110-140
	Establishes new energy-efficiency standards for appliances and lighting products	110-140

Continued

Table B-2.   Continued

Enacted Private-Sector Mandates With Estimated Costs That Exceed the Statutory Threshold, 1996 to 2014

Topic	Description of Mandate	Public Law Number[a]
Finance	Imposes new requirements on credit agencies, lenders, and merchants that handle credit transactions	108-159
	Requires certain depository institutions to pay higher premiums for deposit insurance	109-171, 111-22
	Imposes new requirements on issuers of credit cards and gift cards	111-24
Food Safety	Requires facilities that manufacture, process, pack, receive, or hold food for consumption to register every two years with the Secretary of Health and Human Services, to comply with more frequent inspections, and to pay any fees associated with reinspection or recall	111-353
	Requires entities that manufacture, process, pack, transport, distribute, receive, hold, or import articles of food to comply with new recordkeeping and safety standards, new science-based production and harvesting standards, and new protections for employees	111-353
	Requires owners, operators, and agents of facilities that manufacture, process, pack, or hold food to comply with new recordkeeping and safety standards, particularly in the case of foods determined to pose a high risk for contamination	111-353
Government Fees	Requires companies and other entities to pay certain fees when filing a petition for an H-1B visa	108-447
	Imposes fees on holders and applicants of patents and trademarks	108-447, 110-161, 111-8, 111-45, 111-117, 112-29
	Imposes a surcharge on the filing fee for passport applications	109-167, 112-74, 113-6, 113-76, 113-235
	Extends customs user fees	108-121, 108-357, 110-138, 110-246, 110-436, 111-124, 111-171, 111-227, 111-291, 111-344, 112-41, 112-42, 112-163, 113-67, 113-159
	Authorizes the Federal Deposit Insurance Corporation to assess fees on the financial industry to recover the cost of liquidating financial institutions	111-203
	Increases the merchandise-processing fee collected on most imported goods	112-40, 112-41
Health Care	Requires health insurers to improve portability and continuity of health insurance coverage	104-191
	Requires certain health plans to provide for minimum-length maternity stays	104-204
	Imposes requirements on private health insurance providers under the Medicare program	105-33

Continued

Enacted Private-Sector Mandates With Estimated Costs That Exceed the Statutory Threshold, 1996 to 2014

Topic	Description of Mandate	Public Law Number[a]
Health Care (Continued)	Requires parity in insurance coverage for mental health and other medical benefits	107-147, 108-197, 110-343
	Prohibits providers of group health coverage from offering incentives to military retirees to decline enrollment in a group health plan in favor of relying on the military's health care program	109-364
	Modifies requirements and conditions of continued coverage under the Consolidated Omnibus Budget Reconciliation Act for certain employers who offer group health insurance	111-5
	Requires health insurance plans (including self-insured plans) to comply with new standards for extending coverage to beneficiaries and their dependents	111-148
	Imposes notice and reporting requirements on health insurance plans (including self-insured plans), employers, and other private entities	111-148
	Requires employers to pay an excise tax on employer-sponsored health coverage defined as having high costs	111-148
	Requires health insurance plans (including self-insured plans) to pay an annual fee based on the average number of people covered by the policy	111-148
	Requires individuals to obtain acceptable coverage	111-148
	Imposes additional fees on health insurance providers and on manufacturers and importers of brand-name drugs and certain medical devices	111-148
	Requires private entities that handle health information to comply with new regulations	111-148
	Requires grandfathered health care plans to comply with new standards for extending health insurance coverage to beneficiaries and their dependents	111-152
	Imposes additional fees on health insurance providers and on manufacturers and importers of brand-name drugs; taxes sales of certain medical devices	111-152
	Extends the period during which insurers have to cover certain care provided by the Department of Veterans Affairs to veterans with conditions related to military service	113-175
Housing	Requires Fannie Mae and Freddie Mac to contribute to a fund for affordable housing programs	110-289
Immigration	Imposes requirements on sponsors of immigrants	104-208
Minimum Wage	Increases the minimum wage paid by employers	104-188, 110-28

Continued

Enacted Private-Sector Mandates With Estimated Costs That Exceed the Statutory Threshold, 1996 to 2014

Topic	Description of Mandate	Public Law Number[a]
Motor Vehicles	Imposes new safety requirements on manufacturers of automobiles	107-318, 110-189
	Expands safety requirements for commercial motor carriers	109-59
	Establishes new standards for corporate average fuel economy standards for motor vehicles	110-140
	Requires manufacturers of child safety seats, agricultural equipment, motor vehicles, and vehicle parts to comply with new safety standards	112-141
Motorcoaches	Establishes standards for motorcoach safety	112-141
Online Shopping Security	Requires Internet sellers of goods or services that require consumers to opt out of receiving additional goods or services to provide new and more detailed information about those options to the consumer; prohibits Internet sellers from disclosing the financial information of their customers to any third party	111-345
Pharmaceuticals and Medical Devices	Requires drug manufacturers, at the request of the Food and Drug Administration, to conduct studies to determine the safety and efficacy of drugs and biological products for use in children and to develop appropriate formulations	108-155
	Extends user fees for manufacturers of prescription drugs and medical devices	110-85, 112-144, 112-193
	Prevents manufacturers of generic or biosimilar versions of a drug from selling those products by granting periods of market exclusivity for certain types of drugs	112-144
	Regulates the sale, distribution, and use of selected synthetic drugs	112-144
	Requires dispensers (primarily pharmacies) to pay licensing fees and monitor the movement of prescription drugs through the drug distribution system	113-54
	Regulates 25 new compounds and any compounds found to be structurally similar as anabolic steroids under the Controlled Substances Act	113-260
Pipeline Safety	Requires operators of transmission pipelines for natural gas in areas at risk of significant damage from spills to confirm safe operating pressures for pipelines and adhere to testing regulations	112-90
Rail Transportation	Requires railroads and bus services to implement security plans and conduct security training	110-53
	Requires railroads to develop and install train control technology	110-432

Continued

Table B-2.   Continued

Enacted Private-Sector Mandates With Estimated Costs That Exceed the
Statutory Threshold, 1996 to 2014

Topic	Description of Mandate	Public Law Number[a]
Retirement	Increases required contributions for retirement	105-33
	Increases certain premiums to be paid to the Pension Benefit Guaranty Corporation by sponsors of single-employer and multiemployer defined benefit pension plans	109-171, 112-141, 113-67
	Shortens the schedule for vesting in private retirement funds	109-280
Revenue-Raising Provisions	Requires individuals or businesses to pay more in taxes	104-188, 104-193, 105-2, 105-34, 105-178, 105-206, 105-277, 106-170, 107-147, 108-357, 109-222 (3 mandates), 110-28, 110-140, 110-343 (6 mandates), 111-3, 111-5, 111-12, 111-69, 111-92 (2 mandates), 111-116, 111-147 (2 mandates), 111-148, 111-152 (2 mandates), 111-240, 112-9
Telecommunications	Requires carriers to provide interconnection and universal service and to block certain programs	104-104
	Prohibits the use of a spectrum by extending the deadline for the transition to digital television	111-4
	Requires broadcasters to move channels within the broadcasting spectrum and requires cable companies to carry certain channels	112-96
Tobacco Products	Imposes fees on manufacturers and importers of tobacco products	108-357, 111-31

Source: Congressional Budget Office.

Notes: This table shows the mandates identified by the Congressional Budget Office or the Joint Committee on Taxation (JCT) at the time they were considered or enacted. JCT examines the tax provisions of legislation to identify federal mandates and estimate their costs. Such information is incorporated into CBO's mandate statements.

The list of enacted private-sector mandates with costs exceeding the threshold is not necessarily comprehensive for the 1996–2001 period. Each year during that time, CBO analyzed the status of mandates in legislation that it had reviewed during the previous year to determine whether those mandates had been enacted. Some mandates that were enacted were not considered by a committee during the legislative process and thus might not have been reviewed by CBO. To address that issue, in 2002, CBO began to review all public laws enacted each year to determine whether they contained private-sector mandates. The table shows the mandates identified by CBO at the time they were considered or enacted.

a. Each public law listed contains one mandate unless noted otherwise